The Nature Kid's Guide to

FLAMINGOS

DAVID ANDERSON

LP Media Inc. Publishing
Text copyright © 2026 by LP Media Inc.
All rights reserved.

For information address LP Media Inc. Publishing,
30012 Variolite St NW, Princeton MN 55371
www.lpmedia.org

Publication Data

Flamingos
The Nature Kid's Guide to Flamingos — First edition.

Summary: "Learn all about Flamingos, the Nature Kid Way"
— Provided by publisher.

ISBN: 979-8-89818-107-9

[1. Flamingos – Non-Fiction] I. Title.

Title: The Nature Kid's Guide to Flamingos

CONTENTS

SALTY SHALLOWS

Some flamingo lakes are so salty that the water can sting human skin. Flamingos have tough skin on their legs. This protects them from the harsh water.

Squawk! A pink flamingo stands in shallow water. It looks for food.

Flamingos live in warm, sunny places. They love shallow lakes and muddy flats. The water is often salty or full of minerals. Most animals cannot live in water like this.

These pink birds wade in calm, still pools. The sun beats down on open land. There are no trees nearby. The mud is soft and wet.

Flamingos need this special water to find food. They need flat, muddy spots to build nests. The warm, salty shallows are just right for them.

FLAMINGO FINDER

The largest flamingo groups are found in East Africa, where millions gather together.

Splash! A flamingo walks through a warm lake. Its pink feathers glow.

Flamingos live on many continents.

Greater flamingos live in Africa. They also live in Europe and Asia. You can see them in Kenya and Spain.

Lesser flamingos live in Africa too. They stay near lakes. You find them in Kenya and Tanzania.

Andean flamingos live high up. They live in the Andes Mountains. This is in South America. Chilean flamingos live lower down. They live in Chile and Argentina.

American flamingos live in Florida. They also live in the Caribbean.

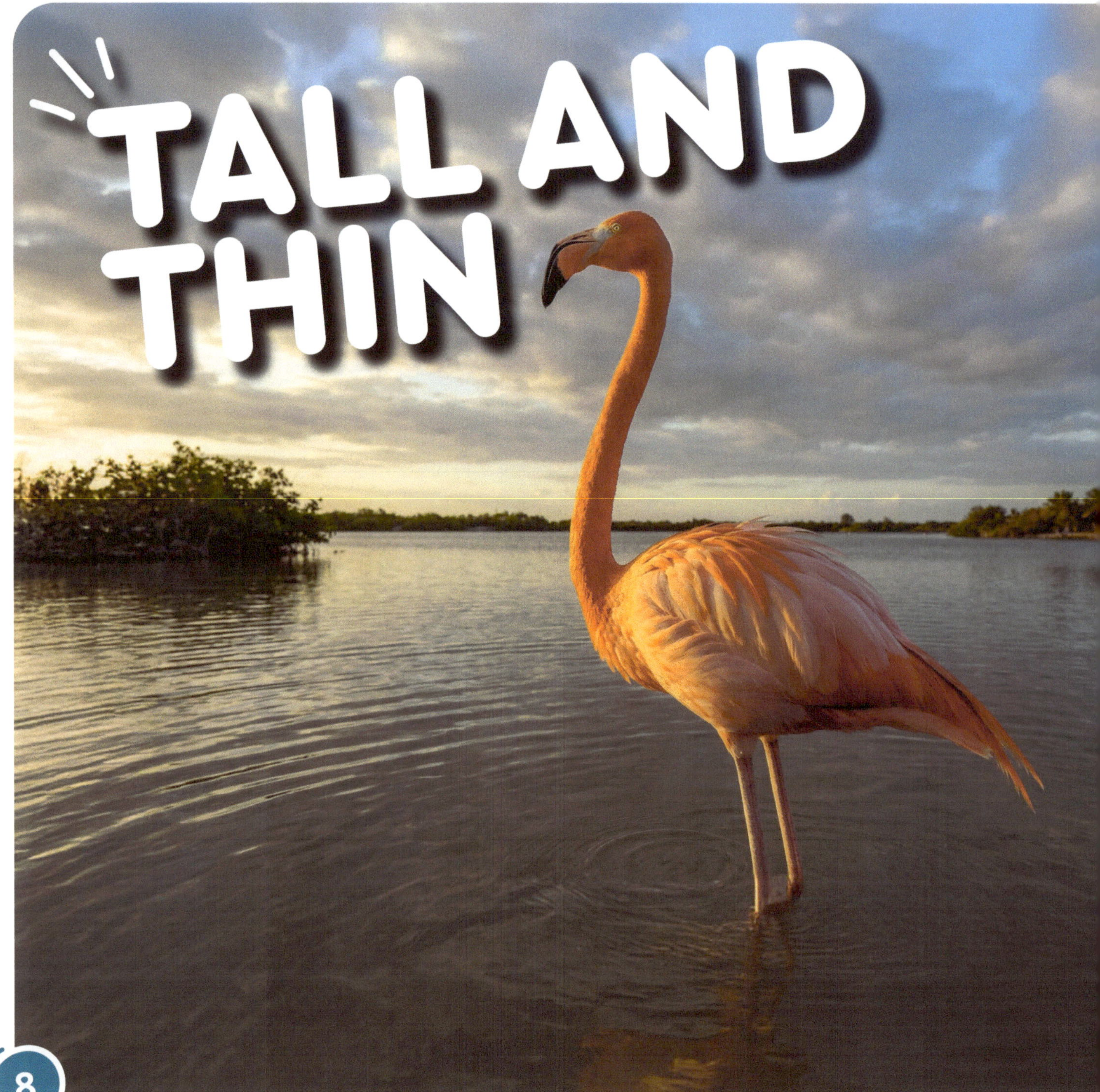
TALL AND
THIN

Whoosh! A tall flamingo stretches its long neck high.

Flamingos are tall birds. They can stand four to five feet high. That is taller than many young children!

These birds have very long legs. Their legs can be longer than their bodies. This helps them wade in deep water.

Flamingos are thin and light. A big flamingo weighs only about nine pounds. Their hollow bones keep them light enough to fly.

A flamingo's neck has 19 bones. A human neck has only 7. That's why they bend so well!

BENDY BODIES

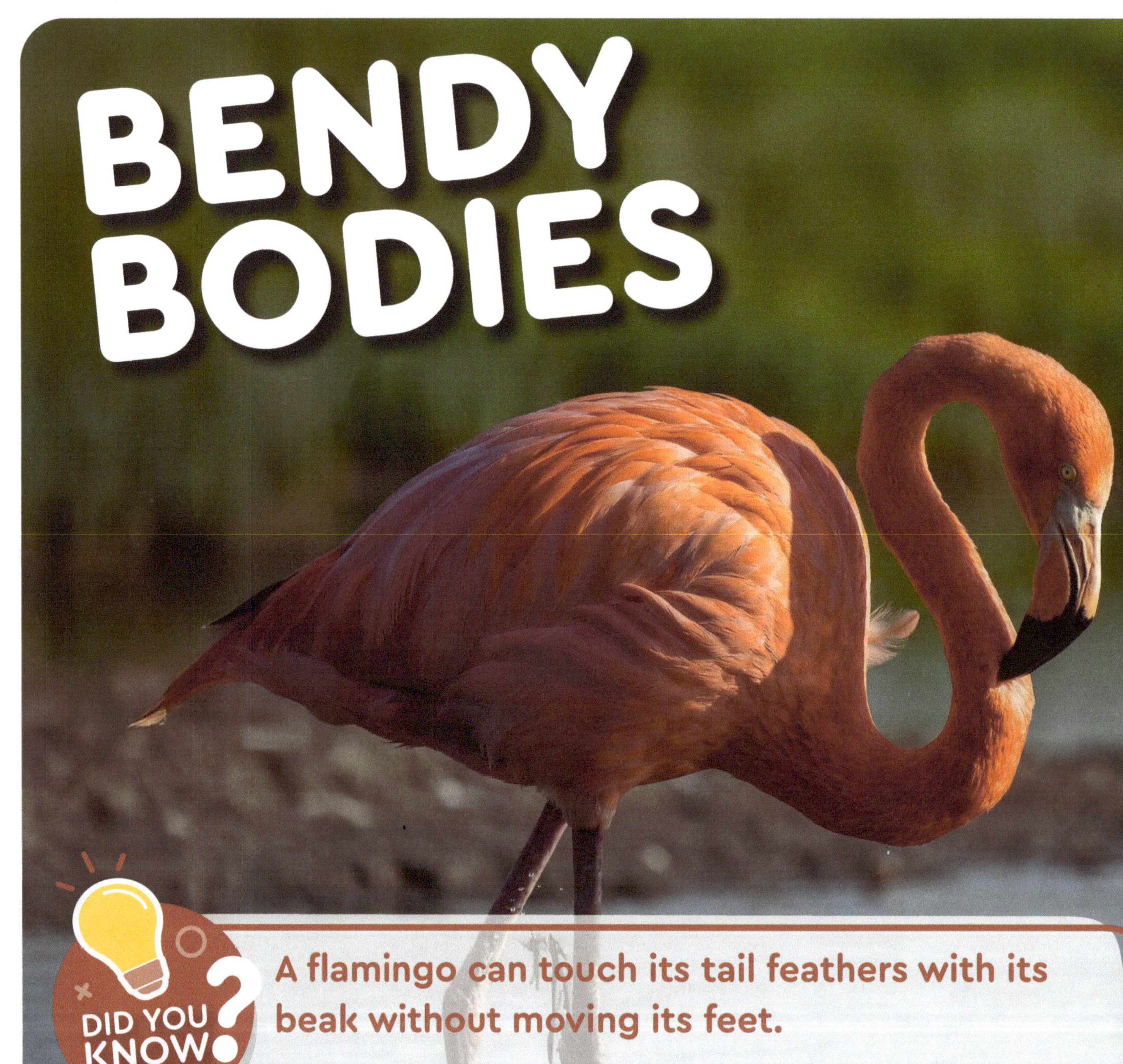

Snap! A flamingo bends its long neck into a tight loop.

Flamingos have very flexible necks. Their long necks have nineteen bones, which lets them twist and turn in many ways.

Their legs look like they bend backward. But that joint is really their ankle! The true knee is hidden under their feathers.

Flamingos can turn their heads upside down to eat with their curved beaks. They also rest their heads on their backs when they sleep. This keeps them warm and cozy.

SUPER
SENSES

Click! A flamingo snaps its beak shut fast. It just caught a tasty snack.

Flamingos have good eyesight. They can see danger from far away. Their eyes sit on the sides of their head.

These birds hear well too. They listen for calls from other flamingos. Each bird has its own special voice.

Flamingos also find food by feeling for it with their beak in the water.

Flamingos can close their nostrils to keep out mud and water.

STAY SAFE

Honk! A flamingo calls out loud. Danger is near the flock!

Flamingos stay safe in groups. Many eyes watch for predators. When one bird sees danger, it honks to warn the others.

Their pink color comes from food. This bright color helps keep them safe. In a big flock, it is hard to pick out just one bird. Predators get confused by all the pink.

They also have strong wings which can carry them away from danger fast.

Andean flamingos have yellow legs and black toes. Their bright colors help scientists tell them apart from other flamingos.

PINK FOOD

Carrots, pumpkins, and sweet potatoes have carotenoids too!

Crunch! A flamingo eats tiny pink shrimp. These little snacks are tasty!

Flamingos eat tiny animals and plants. They find shrimp and snails in the water. They eat algae too. These foods have special colors in them called **carotenoids**.

These colors make flamingos pink! Without this food, they would be white. Or they would be gray. Baby flamingos are born gray. They turn pink as they eat more.

Some foods make dark pink. Some foods make light pink. That is why some flamingos are bright red. Others are pale pink.

FILTER FEEDERS

Swoosh! A flamingo swings its head underwater to find food.

Flamingos are **filter feeders**. They strain water through their beaks to eat. Their beaks have tiny rows inside. These rows are called **lamellae**. They work like a strainer.

A flamingo dips its head upside down. It sucks in water and mud. Then it pushes it all out. Its tongue does the work. The lamellae trap food inside.

This happens very fast. A flamingo pumps water many times each second.

Blue whales are the biggest filter feeders. They can gulp enough water to fill a pool!

WATCH OUT

A Marabou stork stalks the lagoon. It spots baby flamingos.

Flamingos do not have many predators, but there are still dangers. Maribou storks hunt babies and eggs. These birds wait until the parents aren't watching.

Eagles and big cats can hurt them. Jackals and hyenas hunt near the shore.

Eggs and chicks are in the most danger. Gulls and vultures steal eggs from nests when parents are not watching.

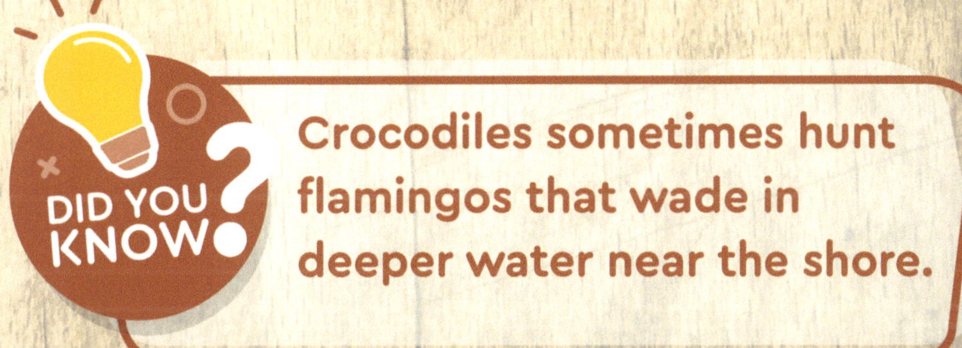

FLY AWAY

Flap! A flamingo lifts off from the water. Its wings stretch wide.

Flamingos can fly up to 40 miles per hour. These pink birds are fast fliers. They use their big wings to soar through the sky.

When a predator comes close, the whole flock takes off together. Hundreds of birds fill the sky at once.

Flying takes a lot of work. Flamingos run on water to take off. They flap hard to get into the air.

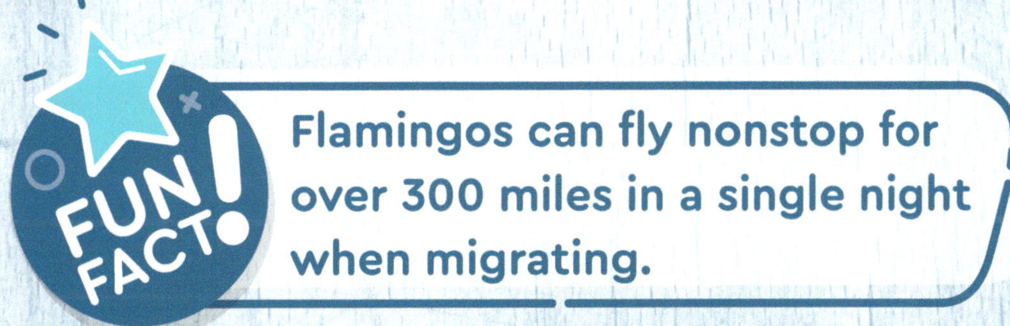

LEGGY LEAPS

Stomp! A flamingo runs across the mud on its long legs.

Flamingos have very long legs. Their legs help them wade in deep water. They can stand up to their bellies!

Flamingos can run on land too. They take big steps. Their skinny legs move fast. Their webbed toes help them balance.

Sometimes flamingos even run on top of the water. This helps them take off and fly!

A flamingo's leg has a backward-bending joint. This is actually its ankle, not its knee.

LAKE LIFE

Flamingos can drink boiling hot water from geysers! Their tough throats handle extreme heat.

Chirp! The sun rises over the lake, and flamingos wake up to start the day.

Flamingos can be active during the day and at night. They spend many hours eating. They also use their beaks to clean their feathers.

These birds rest in the afternoon heat. They often stand on one leg while resting. This helps them stay cool.

Flamingos also bathe in fresh water. They shake their wings to get clean. Staying clean keeps their feathers healthy.

FLOCK
TOGETHER
28

Grunt! Thousands of flamingos crowd together at the lake.

Flamingos live in big groups called flocks. Some flocks have thousands of birds. Living together helps them stay safe.

Flamingos make lots of noise. They honk and call to each other all day long.

These birds do many things together. They eat, sleep, and preen as a group. A flock is never quiet!

Flamingos in a flock often move their heads and march together, like a dance.

DANCE
PARTY

Thump! Flamingos stomp their feet in the mud together.

Flamingos dance in big groups. They march in lines and bob their heads up and down. Many birds move together at the same time.

They also stretch their wings wide. They twist their necks from side to side too. These moves show off their bright pink feathers.

Flocks keep dancing together for weeks. This happens before nesting season begins.

Male and female flamingos dance the same way. Scientists cannot tell them apart!

FLUFFY CHICKS

Peep! A fuzzy gray chick sits on a mud nest. It calls for food.

Flamingo chicks hatch from eggs. They are covered in soft gray or white down. Their beaks are also straight and pink.

Chicks stay in the nest for about one week. Both parents feed them a special red liquid from their throats.

Young flamingos join big groups called **creches**. In these groups, thousands of chicks waddle together. Parents find their own chick by its call.

PARENT
POWER

Squeak! A parent flamingo feeds its hungry chick some milk.

Both flamingo parents take care of their chick. They take turns sitting on the egg before it hatches. This keeps the egg warm and safe.

Parents make a special red liquid called **crop milk** from their throats. This milk is full of fat and protein.

Mom and dad both make crop milk. They feed their chick for about two months. The chick grows strong on this rich food.

A chick's pink beak turns black after about a week of life.

SMART FLAMINGOS

Splash! A flamingo dips its curved beak into the water.

Flamingos have smart ways to stay safe. They live in big groups. Many eyes watch for danger.

Their long legs help them walk in lakes. The salty water keeps bad animals away.

Flamingos can fly fast to get away. They run on the water first. Then they go up into the sky.

Flamingos often live in lakes so salty that few other animals can survive there. This keeps them safer from predators.

FLAMINGO SPOTTING

Splash! A flamingo lands in shallow water.

People go far to see wild flamingos. They travel to far away countries where flamingos live.

Kids can see flamingos at zoos too. This is much easier than a big trip! Zoos keep flamingos in special areas. The birds have ponds with still, shallow water. Zoos make it feel like home. You can see the bright pink feathers up close. Many zoos have signs that teach about flamingos. Some even let kids feed them!

FUN FACT!

Flamingos often stand on one leg. Scientists think this helps them stay warm.

GLOSSARY

carotenoids
Special colors in food that turn flamingos pink.

lamellae
Tiny rows inside a flamingo's beak that work like a strainer to catch food.

filter feeders
Animals that eat by straining water to catch tiny bits of food.

creches
Big groups where baby flamingos stay together.

crop milk
A special liquid that parent flamingos make in their throats to feed their babies.